The Successful Young Entrepreneur

The Successful Young Entrepreneur

Become One Even If You Have A Job!

Buhle Dlamini

Also by Buhle Dlamini

Godly Generation

Young & Able- Activating Your God Given Potential While Young

Balance In The Workplace (Audio book)

Invest In Yourself & Win

The
Successful
Young
Entrepreneur

Become One Even If You Have A Job

Buhle Dlamini

Young & Able Publishing
www.youngable.com

144044850X

This book is dedicated to my wife Stacey who supports me with everything she's got, my kids Bijou, Nhlanhla and Trinity who bring so much joy to my life, my extended family who are such a great bunch and the Young & Able Team who continuously inspire me to be the best I can be.

CONTENTS

CONTENTS

The
Successful
Young
Entrepreneur

Become One Even If You Have A Job

Buhle Dlamini

> "Going into business for yourself, becoming an entrepreneur, is the modern-day equivalent of pioneering on the old frontier."
>
> Paula Nelson

Introduction:

Read This Book And Change Your Net Worth

*I*f you were given a choice between determining your own future income or have someone decide for you, what would you chose? What a dumb question you may think to yourself, of course anyone would choose the former. But the reality is that everyday people, maybe even you have already chosen the latter.

Daily, without thinking twice about it many young, energetic, gifted and full of ideas young people around the world trade their time for a meager pay and a sense of false security. I write this book for anyone out there who's ever thought of becoming an entrepreneur but for some reason has not come around to doing it. Even if you have a job you can change your life by choosing to take the road that few dare to tread.

Most young entrepreneurs are in business to pursue a certain lifestyle and not merely to have a new job. Some entrepreneurs fancy waking up at 10 in the morning, having a nice long breakfast before checking their messages and getting online in their home office and start making money in the PJ's.

While other entrepreneurs fancy the high-rise office downtown with a PA, silk suits, imported cars and the works. No matter what your fancy may be the reality is that entrepreneurship gives you a choice,

> "The entrepreneur is our visionary, the creator in each of us. We're born with that quality and it defines our lives as we respond to what we see, hear, feel, and experience. It is developed, nurtured, and given space to flourish or is squelched, thwarted, without air or stimulation, and dies."
>
> **Michael Gerber**

because it gives you the ability to generate your own income your way.

A successful young entrepreneur then is not just defined by the size of the business or the number of people working for him/her. A successful entrepreneur is one that is able to generate income while enjoying life on one's terms. Successful young entrepreneurs are no longer bound by limits of their educational backgrounds, the geographical context they find themselves in or even their network. In the globalised world we now live in young entrepreneurs launch their business even before finishing school and have a thriving clientele around the world.

You are no longer bound by space and time, nor do you need to have physical products to start a business. You can sell ideas and make more money than you would by pedaling hundreds of physical products a day for your boss.

All you need to know is where to start, what to do and how to do it. That idea you have had in your mind can turn out to be the one that sends you to the big time. The only question is "Are you willing to change your life for better? Or are you content letting others determine your future?

This book will help you answer that question while giving you practical guidance on what you need to do to become The Successful Young Entrepreneur. The choices you make while reading this book can highly increase your chances of success as a young entrepreneur. The advice given here can also assist you in finally making the decision to become that which you have been waiting for your whole life.

The ones who succeed are the ones who know how to seize the opportunity of a lifetime in the lifetime of that opportunity. I hope that you will seize your opportunity too as you read and that it will significantly change your net worth and enrich your life in more ways than you ever thought possible. Read on and change your life!

> "The entrepreneur always searches for change, responds to it, and exploits it as an opportunity."
>
> **Peter Drucker**

Chapter 1:

Change Your Mind Set

At this point most entrepreneurial books launch into a myriad of qualities that entrepreneurs have and that you will need to succeed in business. While this might fill a couple of pages and help me to finish this book quicker I do not see how it can change a sloppy guy and make him cleaner and more acceptable to certain customers.

I think that entrepreneurship is not about trying to fit into some mold that has been predetermined by some business guru somewhere. It is quite the opposite, it's about changing everything you've been told.

It's about going out there and creating your own way to succeed that complements your skills and abilities for the market you want to serve.

It's time for you to change your mind set because becoming an entrepreneur is about a state of mind, it's a way being. Entrepreneurship is not a destination it is a state of being. If you decide to be an entrepreneur today that's what you become and your actions that follow based on that decision shape your future for the rest of your life.

> **"I wanted to be an editor or a journalist, I wasn't really interested in being an entrepreneur, but I soon found I had to become an entrepreneur in order to keep my magazine going."**
>
> **Richard Branson**

Many successful young entrepreneurs quickly realise that becoming an entrepreneur is more about pursuing a dream and a passion than it is about having a new job description. You do have to get over a certain mindset that has been passed on to you by being part of the herd in society. You have to let go of some limiting ideas that have been passed down to you through the generations. Here are some familiar ones you might have to get over:

Entrepreneurs Are A Special Breed Of People: This message has been passed to us in subtle and sometimes not so subtle ways. The problem with this is that it is not true; no two entrepreneurs are exactly the same. Some entrepreneurs are ruthless, cut-throat people who will talk a poor mother out of the last money she has for her kids, while others will go out of their way to make sure that their customer always wins. They are both entrepreneurs but they don't share the same outlook. Anyone can be an entrepreneur, even you!

You Need A Lot Of Money To Be An Entrepreneur: When I started my first business I had a job that paid me just enough to stay alive and get to work everyday, that's another definition of JOB – Just Over Broke. I did not wait for everything to fall into place, while I was still just-over-broke; I started planning my business and used whatever I had to make it happen. It 's amazing how the little that I had grew to become a multi million rand enterprise that now provides employment to others. Stop thinking you need money to be a successful entrepreneur because it 'ain't true'.

Only The Fearless And Brave Can Be Entrepreneurs: It is not the lack of fear that makes successful entrepreneurs to leave their jobs for an unknown future of running their own business. It is acting in spite of fear that makes them succeed. Nelson Mandela once said "I learned that courage was not the absence of fear, but the triumph over it. The brave man is not he who does not feel afraid, but he who conquers that fear." Which leads me to believe that it is possible to overcome the paralyzing fear of failure and I have proven it over and over again in my own life. Everyone, even the ones who are very good at hiding it, get afraid. We all fear that if we try something bold, something extraordinary we will fail miserably. Our minds quickly run to all that could go wrong and when we choose to dwell on those thoughts then sure enough we find ourselves paralyzed to take the next step.

So do not let these limiting thoughts and myths about entrepreneurship keep you from joining with millions of other young entrepreneurs who are shaping the world and changing their lives. Decide to become an entrepreneur and let your ideas and your feet take you to your own unique destination.

> "Shoot for the moon. Even if you miss, you'll land among the stars."
>
> **Les Brown**

Chapter 2:

Where To From Here?

Well, hopefully you have decided to become a successful young entrepreneur and understand that you can be one but now what? Where does one go from here? Deciding where to go is just as important as deciding to go in the first place. Many entrepreneurs fail at this point, by not choosing carefully the direction of their venture, which has to be intricately linked with what they want to do deep down, they soon flounder and fail.

So let's start with you and your strengths. You may already have a business idea; you may already know your strengths. But, you may not have thought about how to apply your strengths to a sound business plan or how to structure your future business. It is important that you focus firstly on yourself not on what you think you should be but on

> "The way to get started is to quit talking and begin doing."
>
> **Walt Disney**

what you already are and already have. This was a critical step in my own entrepreneurial journey, I had to stop and ask myself some hard questions to get a handle on what I could do best

Answer the following questions from three perspectives: Personal/Hobbies, Professional and Financial:

- What makes you really happy?
- What do you enjoy doing?
- What are a couple of things that you are really good at?
- What do others often ask you to do and you like doing it?
- What do you have the most experience doing?

List goals (personal, financial, professional):

- Short-term goals: Goals for the next 3-12 months
- Mid-term goals: Goals for the next 1-3 years
- Long-term goals: Goals for the next 3-6 years

By now you should start to see some sort of pattern into how you're wired. You should also be narrowing down some sort of business idea/s and/or path that you should follow. Developing some sort of ideas, based on your strengths and goals, on how you want to conduct your business (e.g., work from home, part-time while keeping current job, retail store, client interaction, over the internet business etc).

For instance, do you like working with children? If you do, you may want to think about starting your own daycare center or pre-school. If you have a little bit of a teaching background the better your chances of success. Another example can involve your love for

> **"There are a lot of things that go into creating success. I don't like to do just the things I like to do. I like to do things that cause the company to succeed. I don't spend a lot of time doing my favorite activities."**
>
> **Michael Dell**
>
> Founded Dell Computers with $1000 and creating a net worth of $20 billion USD before the age of 40.

pets. Do you enjoy working with pets? If you do, you may want to think about starting your own pet supply store, dog grooming business, or pet sitting service. Starting a small business based on something that you not only know, but also love, will up your chances of your business being a successful one.

Although it is advised that you choose and start a small business based around something that you know and love, that shouldn't be the only factor that you examine. You also need to examine your competition. When running an online business for example, you can expect to receive a lot of competition online, that's just how the Internet works.

When it comes to starting your own local business, you will want to start a business that has a relatively small amount of competition. In fact, the smaller the amount of competition, the better it will be for you and your business. For instance, if you live in a small town and there are already two or three pet sitting services available, it is advised that you do not start another one, as the demand will not be as high as the supply.

Most people have some type of business idea that they think is wonderful and that they think could be the next Google or FaceBook. But few people actually take the time to sit back and think about the reality of starting a business or the feasibility of their idea. The most important question to answer at this stage is, "Can this business make money?" The next question should be "How will it make money?"

How are the other similar businesses in your field of interest doing? Ask these questions and look for answers:

• Is there a growing need/desire for the products or services that you want to sell?
• Are similar businesses in my field of interest growing, slowing, or stagnating?
• Are similar businesses going out of business?
• Can I offer something unique that no one else is doing yet? (E.g. better price/service, new technology or way of doing things)
• Who will buy from me, my target market/customer?

Based on the answers you reach you can then choose to proceed. Above everything else the most important thing to remember is : start with something you have a high chance of succeeding in. If you start by wanting to be the next Bill Gates and ask your local bank for a 5 million dollar loan, chances are you wont succeed. But if you go for achievable smaller goals first they will boost and give you confidence for the big fish.

> "The general who wins the battle makes many calculations in his temple before the battle is fought. The general who loses makes but few calculations beforehand."
>
> **Sun Tzu**

Chapter 3:

Creating A System For Success

Many ideas die as nothing more than great ideas because they have no clear system or plan to them. Sometimes the most vivid ideas in your mind at 2 o clock in the morning when you can't sleep turn out to be nothing more than wishful thinking while others with proper systems to them turn nobodies into millionaires.

It is not how brilliant an idea is that makes successful young entrepreneurs successful but rather it is the clarity of the system of the idea. This clarity leads you to know what exactly will be needed to make your business a success and to craft a business plan. I am not a big fan of business plans because many people just go off and pay some consultants to write a document. A business plan is first and foremost an explanation of the system you plan to follow to your success.

So here is what I suggest you do at this stage: Draw your idea as a diagram on a piece of paper outlining the steps involved leading to money in your pocket. Here is my example I used to launch my online website builder company:

Service Offered:
Online Website Builder and Hosting For Small Businesses (clear service and customer base)

↓

How Is It Offered:
Resell Hosting & Online Website Builder From International Supplier (lower price and maintenance, no servers and only buy from supplier what we sell)

↓

How Do We Access Customers:
Market the website online and offline ads on small business publications (targeted marketing guaranteeing a reasonable response)

↓

What Is The Process:
Customers sign up online, fill a debit order and start building their website online. (No need to be in physical contact with customers everything is automated even if I'm sleeping)

↓

How Do We Get The Money:
Debit Order Mandates are on file and monthly a batch is submitted and we get paid automatically (guaranteed income, no complicated systems to follow)

It is that simple! Creating a system is more for the entrepreneur than it is for a business plan document that is sent to the bank. When you have a business system you can draw up the business plan with all those fancy words and headings, but it is the system that you need to know in your head. As the business grows you will know where people you might employ fit into that system.

You will need a business plan for sure but for that you can use business-planning software that literally guides you through the steps. You can visit YoungEntrepreneur.co.za for some of the recommended business plan software. Clarify your system now and start your business.

"A brand for a company is like a reputation for a person. You earn reputation by trying to do hard things well."

Jeff Bezos
Founder of Amazon.com

Chapter 4:

Creating A Brand For Your Success

*T*he next step on your journey is more about clarity of what you stand for as much as it is about getting noticed. Successful entrepreneurs know and understand that running a business is about being clear about the value you will bring to your customers.

Think of Dell- affordable computers assembled and delivered according to customer specifications. Think of MacDonald's- affordable fast food delivered in the same fashion and quality whether in New York or Mumbai. Think of Chuck Norris – Good butt-kicking with a high moral ground and cowboy hat to go with it.

Is my point getting through? Branding is important for the entrepreneur and his customers. When you don't know what you stand for it makes no sense incorporating and hanging your sign above the door. Getting a clear brand for your business is about being able to clearly describe what you do to a stranger in a few moments it takes to get to your destination on the elevator.

Many new entrepreneurs dread the question "So what do you do?" But your ability to clearly answer without a lot of detail will also determine how you deliver on that promise to your customers. Think of the example of the business I shared with you in the previous chapter and look at the following elevator pitch for it:

"We offer small businesses an ability to build and host their websites online at a fraction of the cost and time."

This pitch easily leads to other questions that give you the opportunity to tell more but even if no questions follow the brand is clear enough.

Developing a brand is much more than just deciding on a name or picking some colors. A brand is the sum of all you do. It's derived from all your touch points with your customers and prospects.

Developing a brand requires having a plan that consistently communicates what your business is and does, along with your distinct attributes, image, and personality.

We choose one company's product or service over another's because it offers a benefit. This is the company's competitive advantage and feeds to it's brand. Standing out, pushing past the competition and then staying ahead of the competition are all important branding components of a successful business. To do that, you need to be clear on the unique benefits you offer.

Ask yourself, why do people buy from you? Does it make them feel good? Does it save them money? Does it make them smarter or help them avoid pain?

List at least five features of your product or service. Think about what you have that's the biggest, quickest, cheapest, most up-to-date or friendliest. Fill in these blanks to get started:

1. We have the largest _____ in the industry.

2. Our _____ is the quickest around.

3. We provide the cheapest _____ for our customers.

4. Our _____ and process is the most up-to-date technologically.

5. We pride ourselves in having the most user-friendly _____.

For each of the features listed above, state what it does for the customer. For instance, it may save time, save money, make money, make them healthier, keep inventory low, taste better or be less filling.

Remember only you create and maintain the kind of brand that you can deliver on and that will guarantee ongoing business success. As a professional speaker in my speaking and consulting business I strive to be known as entertaining, educational and motivating at the same time. This creates an expectation for my clients and a target for myself. By clarifying this for myself I am then able to deliver on that consistently and increase my client base. You can do the same for your business right from the beginning and it will serve you greatly in the long term.

> "Corporation: An ingenious device for obtaining profit without individual responsibility."
>
> **Ambrose Bierce**

Chapter 5:

Getting Organised: Business Structure

*T*he structure you choose for your business is just as important to your success as the system you have for it. Whether you have decided to resell e-books, create a new product or be part of a franchise, your business will need to become an entity on its own. You should evaluate the advantages and disadvantages of each business formation, paying special attention to the tax implications and government formalities.

There are different business structures to choose from and each structure will have its own pros and cons and you should pay careful attention to your country's tax laws.

Some forms of business ownership are:

1. **Sole Proprietorship**
2. **Partnership**
3. **Corporation**
4. **Company**

Sole Proprietorship

Sole proprietorship is a popular choice for many new business owners because so little is needed to set it up. Apart from local business licenses, there are minimal government fees and paperwork.

On the other hand, there are also considerable risks to consider—for example, your personal assets are vulnerable to creditors and other liabilities such as lawsuits. You also don't get to take advantage of certain tax breaks that are reserved for more formal business structures such as Corporations or Companies.

Most importantly, as a sole proprietorship, your company name is not protected. In other words, there is nothing to prevent another company from incorporating under your business name.

Partnership

Similar to sole proprietorship, a partnership is extremely easy to set up and maintain, requiring no government fees or annual state paperwork. If you are thinking of setting a business with another person this makes perfect sense. You can combine your skills and experience with someone else and get a business going.

On the downside, you and your partner/s are each held fully responsible for all of your business's debts. This means if you or one of your partners defaults on a business loan, creditors can go after your personal bank accounts, property holdings and other assets to satisfy the entire loan.

As a partnership, you are also at a disadvantage when it comes to raising funds. For example, you cannot raise capital by selling stock, and private investors may be wary of investing in your company without personal liability protection. Finally, just as with sole proprietorships, your company name is not protected. This means any new or existing business could incorporate using your business name.

Corporation (Close Corporation)

Corporations are the standard for many businesses in today's market. This is the form of business I have used for all my business ventures so far. The primary reason is that incorporating shields you and the members of your business from personal liability. In other words, if your business hits hard times, creditors cannot go after your personal assets to make up for any company shortfalls.

But protection from personal liability is not the only benefit that comes with incorporating. The corporate business structure also offers significant tax savings, greater business flexibility, business name protection and increased opportunities for raising capital. You can also buy shelf corporations and change the name for quicker incorporation.

A corporation can have up to 10 members in South Africa and each has a percentage ownership out of 100% and that determines their ownership. This means that individuals can buy ownership and this can provide startup funds if the individuals concerned are able to foot the bill.

One thing to keep in mind - corporations do require some initial set up fees and a certain amount of regular maintenance. For example, you'll have to keep up-to-date corporate records as well as file an annual report with the state.

They also require that you have a financial officer and trust me this is not a bad thing because having someone who has an accounting background will be very helpful anyway. You can find an accountant that will fill this role for you for a very little monthly contribution. As your business grows your accounting needs will also grow and you'll be able to afford more of your accountant's time.

> "We succeed in enterprises which demand the positive qualities we possess, but we excel in those which can also make use of our defects."
>
> Alexis de Tocqueville

Company.

As with a CC, a company is a separate legal entity that can acquire rights and take on obligations in its own name, but which is owned by its shareholders, who can be natural or juristic persons (that is, another company while a CC can not be owned by another company).

The shareholders own shares, but have no obligation to the management of the company, unless they are also appointed as directors.

> **"You don't need to have a 100-person company to develop that idea."**
>
> **Larry Page**
> Google co-founder

The profits belong to the company, which decides how they will be distributed. The debts also belong to the company and not the shareholders. However, in the case of smaller companies, the directors, who are often the main shareholders, also stand surety for the company's debts.

A company pays income tax in its own right at a higher percent of taxable income than other forms business. Shares held at the death of a shareholder are subject to estate duty and CGT (Capital Gain Tax).

No matter what structure you choose for your business remember it's got to work for you the best. You must be clear about the goals of your business and decide which structure is going to serve you best at the time. You can grow from one structure to another as you move up in business.

So go on and get yourself incorporated!

"In the end, the customer doesn't know, or care, if you are small or large as an organisation... she or he only focuses on the garment hanging on the rail in the store."

Giorgio Armani

Chapter 6:

But I Don't Have A Product

One of the biggest challenges in starting and running a successful business is developing and getting the right product or service to offer your clients. Product and service development require long lead times and serious cash at times locking most would be entrepreneurs out of the business game. But in today's world of globalization and easy access to information from around the globe getting a product is no longer impossible.

Today you can start and run a very profitable business enterprise without ever developing a product or service of your own. Here is how you can leverage on other people's products and watch your business grow from nothing to something really profitable.

Different Business-Without-Product Types You Can Start:

Distribution Business

Is there a product that you see a lot of potential for with a certain clientele that is not currently reached? The easiest way to start this form of business is by taking an already available product that you are confident in and ask the company that owns it if you can distribute it for them. The way you make money here is by being a go between, connecting clients with the product owners. Some companies would even deliver the product to your client once the sale has been made. Try and avoid initial overhead costs by not having to buy stock from your supplier but work on pay-as-you go basis.

> "A business is successful to the extent that it provides a product or service that contributes to happiness in all of its forms."
> Mihaly Csikszentmihalyi

Online Distribution and Affiliate Service

The other way of starting a business without a product of your own is by providing an online service that gives a very specific clientele access to the product/service you have sourced. You create a website, market it to your specific audience and get the supplier to send products directly to your clients while you receive payments and keep the profits. This may be more technical but worth it. You can also become an affiliate to high earning products and get money for promoting them.

> **"Thousands of people were producing new Web sites every day. We were just trying to take all that stuff and organize it to make it useful."**
>
> **David Filo**
> Cofounder of Yahoo!

Start A Sales Agency For One Product/Service

If you are good at selling, you can start a service where you sell specific products to a certain market.

You can sell products with a recurring billing and make ongoing profits from the monthly payments of the clients you introduce to the products or service. You also charge a once off sales fee for getting the client in the first place. You can actually grow this agency by getting more agents on a commission basis, this way you will not be stuck with salary overheads.

There are so many other ways you can grow a real successful business over time without ever coming up with a new product or service.

> **"There is always plenty of capital for those who can create practical plans for using it"**
>
> **Napoleon Hill**

Chapter 7:

What About The Money: Capital

    *O*ne of the often cited challenges in starting and running a successful business is getting the necessary capital/money to make money in your own business. This problem is a myth that has stopped many would be entrepreneurs from advancing from the starting blocks.

Real successful young entrepreneurs don't allow a simple thing like money to limit their dream of running a successful business. As I mentioned before it's not about starting with the biggest plans possible but it's about being as practical as possible. There are plenty of businesses you can start without having to sell your soul for capital to a bank or to a venture capital firm.

Of course there will come a time where you will have to approach these beasts but by then you should have learned a thing or two about what it really means to run a business. Your first priority should be to get up and running by building your own business from scratch. This builds the confidence you will need for when you have to go after the big fish.

Most business startup books tell you to have a good business plan and what you need to have in the plan. I am telling you to start a business and make it work first with what you have and when you can predict authentically what is really possible then go for the big cash. The biggest mistake you'll make in business is getting other people's money because you're convinced that you can make something work, only to fall flat on your face.

> "The highest use of capital is not to make more money, but to make money do more for the betterment of life."
>
> Henry Ford

Bootstrapping

Bootstrapping is by far your best chance of succeeding in starting and running your business as far as I am concerned. This is where you the entrepreneur use your own funds to finance your business. But I don't have much, you say. Welcome to the club of many other young entrepreneurs who have gone on to have multi million dollar businesses from scratch. These funds can come from a variety of sources, such as personal savings, credit cards, or by selling off other assets (that souped-up-car parked in your garage) to free up needed cash. This is by far the easiest way to get money; however, it can also be the riskiest. You can loose everything. But that is the beauty of it too. Loosing everything if it's a little and you are young isn't as bad as loosing everything and it belongs to the bank and it's millions.

Friends and Rich Uncles and Aunts

Ever wanted to just go over to your rich family members and hit them up for some cash for your business? Tempting isn't it? But it's risky too. You must walk a very tight rope when going this route; you don't want to exploit the trust these people have in you, but you want to get the financing you need for your business. It can be very damaging if the business goes downhill, these people are some of your closest allies, but borrowing money from them can put a strain on your relationship.

Your most important thing to remember when you go this route is to make sure that you protect relationships at all cost. Have very clear plans on how people will get their money back should you succeed or not this way there will be no sour grapes in the relationship.

Government & SME Grants

If you look carefully you will find that there is a lot of free money floating around for your business in government and other SME (Small Medium Enterprise) Grants. But be warned the journey to getting it might be longer and more costly than what it's worth. Consider this; you apply for 10 thousand to get your business started but end up spending 2 thousand in transport, getting documents drawn up right and other costs. This is ok if you get the money but if you are turned down, you have just lost months of productivity in your business. In effect you are worse off than when you started the process.

Here is what I suggest: apply for grants while you plough ahead with your business. Work hard on making your business work and at the same time try and get as much of the grant money that is available in your line of business. Do not let your hope of getting grant money become your main plan for success. Find out what the requirements are and weigh them up against the final reward if it is worth it, then by all means go for it, if not move on.

> **"Capital isn't that important in business. Experience isn't that important. You can get both of these things. What is important are ideas."**
>
> **Harvey S. Firestone**

Business Bank Loans

Well, I am just going to come out and say it: DON'T DO IT!!! I do not advise this route and that is my opinion. You're young, smart and innovative. Do you really want to tie your future to the bank? I am still reeling from the effects of a student loan, the money they gave me didn't even last a semester but payments lasted much longer and robbed me of my first fruits of my labour. If you have to do this go speak to someone else who will help you sign your life away. However when you have some measure of success under your belt and can predict your business future then it is plausible to ask the bank for assistance in funding your growth.

There are other means of getting funding or capital for your business such as venture capitalists and angel investors. I personally have not had the pleasure of dealing with these creatures although I have heard quite a lot about them. Speak to someone who received funding from either and let them answer your questions before you jump in. You can get money for starting or growing your business but your first resort should be using your own resources for your rocket to take off.

"If you don't act now while it's fresh in your mind, it will probably join the list of things you were always going to do but never quite got around to. Chances are you'll also miss some opportunities."

Paul Clitheroe

Chapter 8:

Finding Your Niche For Success: Business Ideas

To really make it in business you need to find and capitalize on business ideas that are uniquely placed for you and the kind of customers you want to reach. The key lies in your understanding of the key players in this equation, you and your customers. You because your skills, knowledge and abilities will determine what you can offer your customers. Customers because without them and their insatiable appetite for your products or services there will be no business to speak of.

So what are some ideas to consider in crafting your own niche in the market?

Niche Service Business

Starting a service business for a niche or specific audience is one of the easiest routes an entrepreneur can take. This is really about doing some research on a very particular service that you know you can offer to a select group of customers.

Is there something particular that you can do that some people will be willing to pay you money to do? Are you able to get enough people who will need what you can do and can they sustain your business over time? This can be something that will save some people time, something they are willing to outsource and hopefully something they will come back again and again to get from you.

I built a niche business as a professional speaker on business and personal development issues. Because this is a niche business I am able to charge a huge fee for one presentation meaning that I need a few presentations a month to have a thriving business. This is a developed industry with many people offering different kinds of presentations. This means that for me to get a piece of that pie I have to have something fresh and unique to offer so I chose topics about change, future and understanding the new world of customers and employees. Being young myself I can be an authentic voice and I bring humour and entertainment value to my offering.

What area can you bring a niche service offering? Are you a graphic designer with a keen interest in cars? Why not design only for auto dealers or car racing specialists. Or you can do bookkeeping and accounting for florists or landscapers. You can corner a very specific market doing

> **"The entrepreneur in us sees opportunities everywhere we look, but many people see only problems everywhere they look. The entrepreneur in us is more concerned with discriminating between opportunities than he or she is with failing to see the opportunities."**
> **Michael Gerber**

what you love to do. What's great about a niche service business is that you can start with very little or nothing. You can do it while you are working for a boss and only work on your business part time.

Consulting Business

Ever thought of being a consultant? Why not? This is a legitimate way to go into business for yourself that will cost you very little except for the knowledge; experience and training you have already received. What is a consultant any way? The dictionary describes a consultant as "an expert in a particular field who works as an advisor either to a company or to another individual." Whoa! What a goldmine for young entrepreneurs!

With an increasing number of small businesses requiring specific services on an ongoing basis why not take the opportunity to consult for them. This way you don't need a job from any of them they can each pay you a little bit to make up for a very huge payoff for you at the end of the month. The thing about consulting is that when you have more clients than you can service yourself you can hire someone else until you are a fully-fledged consulting firm.

Don't get carried away now, be careful not to be a jack-of-all-trades, choose one specific area and deliver a quality service. Think about becoming a small business software consultant. There are so many software programs out there that are specifically for small businesses from accounting to desktop publishing. Decide what you'll focus on and find out if there are any accreditation courses you can take and whether you can serve as an official distributor as well.

I know of individuals who have studied Human Resources who offer HR services to small businesses that cannot afford a full time HR executive. They have up to 10 clients that pay them double of what one HR executive gets working in one company. Because their clients are small businesses their workload is so minimal you can catch them playing golf most afternoons.

The same can extend to the following services:

- Accounting

- Advertising

- Auditing

- Business writing

- Communications

- Computer consulting

- Editorial services

- Executive search/headhunter firms

- Human resources

- Insurance

- Marketing

- Payroll management

- Public relations

Niche Product For A Niche Market

The most common and easier still route to creating a niche for your success is finding or creating a product for a select group of customers. You need to spend more time researching and calculating with this route. Before going out and buying a garage load of a specific product to sell to your prospects make sure you have done your calculations correctly and can back them up with research. There have been many would-be-millionaires who got caught going this route and never tried business again. When you have your ducks in a row properly and you are certain that you have a winner then go ahead and source the product to sell to your niche market. I have more information in the next chapter about going from idea to product if you are thinking of creating your own product.

"I think it's very important that whatever you're trying to make or sell, or teach has to be basically good. A bad product and you know what? You won't be here in ten years."

Martha Stewart

Chapter 9:

From Idea to Product, Sales and Marketing Success

So many ideas, so few successes! That's how it goes in entrepreneur-land. Many brilliant ideas in young entrepreneurs minds remain just that-brilliant ideas. Very few of them become real products that turn into real sales and result in marketing successes written about in international magazines and turn zeros into heroes overnight.

How can you make sure that you also make it and leave behind the scores of others who have only just dreamt of hitting the big time? There are proven steps that will move you from idea or dream to reality. You will fare much better if you consider these steps than just hoping everything is just going to fall into place all by itself.

Write It Down:

Ever had an idea in the middle of the night when you can't sleep and your creative juices are flowing? You think to yourself at that point 'this must be the best idea in the world, it's going to make me rich!' and then you roll over and fall asleep. If you have a good memory you will capture the essence of what it was but the details might be lost. I now keep a notebook close to me all the time and I use it to document the good ideas I come up with. Write down everything you can think of that relates to your idea/invention, from what it is and how it works to how you'll make and market it.

This step comes in handy for later into your process, as it will offer some guidance into what needs to be done. When the idea is fresh in your mind then your brain is also better equipped to come up with solutions to possible obstacles to making it happen. As you document your idea you also ask yourself some hard questions about it. The questions can range from 'why do I think this idea will work?' To 'who will be the ideal customer and how will they find out about it?'

Get More Than Your Own Opinion:

Have you noticed how your own opinion sounds so much better than everyone else's? That's because it's yours and it will always sound better to you than anybody else's. But if you really want to succeed you've got to ask for other people's opinions on the subject. This is often called

> **The point to remember about selling things is that, as well as creating atmosphere and excitement around your products; you've got to know what you're selling.**
>
> **Stuart Wilde -**

research but really all that it means is that you ask around to validate what you think is a good idea.

If you want to sell something that will make teachers' jobs a little easier then you will do well to ask some teachers if they would be interested in the product or service you want to offer. Ask enough people to make sure that you have a representative analysis of the market. If out of a 100 teachers only 5 are interested in what you want to offer then already the warning bells are ringing loud and clear. Skip this step and you will only have yourself to blame when everything comes crashing down around you.

Padlock Your Idea:

If your idea is worth a lot based on your research and other people's opinion then you better protect it. This is an often-overlooked aspect of product/service development that leaves many smart people crying on the roadside of entrepreneurial success. Go online and research a patent process for your line of product or service and start padlocking your idea from the idea thieves out there.

Assemble A Dream Team:

To make any idea work you are going to need people around you that are going to make it possible. You need to have your own dream team as it were. Stop hyperventilating; you won't have to hire them yet! Ask yourself: What skills am I going to require in making this idea to work?
So start painting your dream team by writing down profiles with required skills and knowledge before you put names next to them. Once you have all your dream team profiles move on to think or ask around for those who can fulfill these roles. Once you have these people, build relationships with them and let them be your go-to people relating to the different areas. Work with them, ask them questions, win their trust and be loyal to them.

At first they will offer advice but as your idea gets wings they will start to offer specific services to you and as time goes on they can become partners, employees and consultants to you. Never underestimate the importance of a dream team they are the ones behind every great invention that you see today. The entrepreneur gets the limelight, book deals and interviews on Oprah. But it is the dream team that makes the product that takes the world by storm a reality.

Design A Prototype/Sample

You better start designing at this point. Get the best but affordable designer to get you started. If your product needs to be manufactured find out where might be the best place to do that. It could happen that you have to manufacture your product in another country to save costs. You can go to Alibaba.com to find out and speak to manufacturers from around

> **"The essence of a successful business is really quite simple. It is your ability to offer a product or service that people will pay for at a price sufficiently above your costs, ideally three or four or five times your cost, thereby giving you a profit that enables you to buy and to offer more products and services."**
>
> **Brian Tracy**

the world. Use your dream team to help design a product that is uniquely yours. Have a prototype that you can test and sample with potential customers. A prototype is a great way to get support from financers and to test whether your ideal customer thinks you've hit the jackpot.

Now To Market!

You now have an idea that is protected, a great dream team behind you and a prototype of a great product loved by all. Now where to from here? To market! To market!

How do you get from prototype product to being in all major shops or written about on Time magazine, well maybe your local newspaper. You need a plan to take you there. Here is what you do:

Create A Sales Plan:
Start by clearly defining your market. Remember all that niche stuff we spoke about earlier? Who is your ideal customer for your product or service? How much do they earn? How can they be reached easily, online, newspaper or phone? How much are they likely to spend on your type of product?

Sales Goals: After answering these questions you can have goals for sales i.e. how many pieces you plan to sell a month to cover your costs and make profit.

Sales Process: A clearly defined process for making a sale. This has to be designed in such a way that it costs you as little as possible to make a sale of each product. You can choose to sell your product only through petrol/gas stations. You'll have to negotiate the rate, get an agreement and get the product to their distribution system. Whatever you decide to do have a clear sales process in place.

Remember to start small and get a record you can use to approach big retailers to carry your product.

Expand & Grow Your Market and Brand:

You have to get people to associate your product or service with a particular brand that you want to build and manage over time. As mentioned in the chapter about branding for success you need to be clear about the customer experience you want to be known for.

To get going on this you can start by selling directly to end users via the web or direct sales. This way you can start creating a customer experience and also grow your market via word of mouth. If people like what you offer and start telling others about it you are on your way.

Get noticed: This may sound pushy, well it is. What's the point of having a great product that nobody knows about? You better get pushy and get people to notice you, there's no point in being shy here. Do something newsworthy to launch your product and tell your local news about it. The wackier the better, the bigger the better, just get noticed. Have a way to capitalize on that attention you get initially. Run a competition linked to your launch so that those who enter stand a chance to win something substantial like a great holiday. People who enter your competition can become your initial marketing base, you've got their details and they know about your product now sell to them!

To avoid loosing momentum plan more things in the pipeline to get you noticed again and again until everyone knows your product and are buying.

You are now in business!

"I'm not sure I knew what an entrepreneur was when I was ten, but I knew that starting little businesses and trying to sell greeting cards or newspapers door-to-door or just vending machine kind of thing is... there's just something very intriguing to me about that."

Steve Case
Founder of America Online AOL

Chapter 10:

What If: FAQ For Young Entrepreneurs

Why don't all books have a-what if chapter? All good websites have a very extensive FAQ page for frequently asked questions about the product or service. I am sure your head is reeling with 101 what-if questions. In this chapter I am not going to answer 101 what-ifs but I will take a crack at 11 for you.

1. What If I Am Scared Of Heights?

Don't start a parachute adventure company because you will definitely not succeed in business. The trick is to stay away from your natural weakness and focus as much energy on building your business around your strengths. This point here brings the downfall of many; don't make a mistake of underestimating your weaknesses.

2. What If I am Terrified Of Selling?

You're not the only one. But if you are in business you've got to sell to someone somewhere. Whether it's selling the business idea to a potential investor or actually selling your product to the end user you better get used to the idea. You can hire someone to become a full time sales person for you but as an entrepreneur you're only in business if you sell, sell, sell. Get some great books on becoming better at sales but remember you've got to sell people yourself first. It's not as bad as it seems and you don't have to be like the sales people who put you off, you can sell differently and naturally.

> "The fact is; everyone is in sales. Whatever area you work in, you do have clients and you do need to sell."
> Jay Abraham

3. What if I Want To Buy A Business?

Not a bad idea! In most cases, buying an existing business is less risky than starting one from scratch. Buying business is just as entrepreneurial as starting one up. You often see businesses in your area that are badly run and you think to yourself "what a gold mine in the wrong hands." An existing business means an existing customer base, monthly cash flow and existing products and services.

On the downside, buying a business is often more costly than starting from scratch. However, it's easier to get financing to buy an existing business than to start a new one. Be careful to do your homework on the business you want to buy. Do you have what it takes to be a winner? In the same way you have to be prepared in starting a business from scratch, you need to have a plan in buying one.

4. What If Nobody Takes Me Seriously?

Well, as a young entrepreneur one of your biggest challenges could be simply getting people to take you seriously. It is hard to gain the trust of most customers in most cases but it can be extra hard if you're young and inexperienced.

Think of Mark Zuckerberg who founded Facebook while he was a student at Harvard University. Facebook received its first investment of US$500,000 (that's half a million!) in June 2004 from PayPal co-founder Peter Thiel; this led to many other investments. Mark had to convince a lot of people along the way, so will you if you are to succeed as an entrepreneur.

> "I've found that luck is quite predictable. If you want more luck, take more chances. Be more active. Show up more often."
>
> Brian Tracy

To increase your chances of being trusted and taken seriously by customers, investors and bankers there are a few things you can do. Start networking with business leaders in your community and industry to learn and share knowledge. In no time you'll be sounding smarter and your confidence will peak. Also commit to offering a quality service every time and that will not only make people take you seriously but it will also enhance your brand.

5. What If I Can't Name My Business?

Naming your business can be a huge challenge because so much of a business's success is dependent on the name. You need to approach the naming of your business from your customers' point of view, it should communicate as well as create interest. The easier it is on the tongue the better, try and think of a name that is memorable. Shorter business names fare better than longer ones and unique ones save your business from being confused with others. Also remember that your name should be able to fit in a domain for your website.

6. What If I Need To Create A Logo

> **"Your premium brand had better be delivering something special, or it's not going to get the business."**
>
> **Warren Buffett**

Your logo gives your customers their first impression of your business. Over time your business logo becomes a critical part of your brand, think of MacDonald's and the golden arches come to mind. A business logo can create loyalty or turn your prospects off so you really cannot skimp on this one. Spend time and money in developing a really professional logo that communicates what you stand for. Be clear about the message you want your logo to communicate, it's no good going to a designer and saying 'make us a good logo'.

Take some time to look at other logos in your line of business and decide which one closely communicates what you want. Make sure your logo is clean and functional there's nothing worse than a busy logo. Remember that your logo colours will affect your business colours going forward. If you do a good job on creating a logo that communicates more than the name of your business you create a brand for your business that will last.

7. What If I Want An E-business?

An ecommerce business is a great way to go for young entrepreneurs. It is much easier to start and has a whole lot less requirements than the brick and mortar kind of business. Starting a business on the Internet might be easier but succeeding in one can be lot trickier. This is mainly because the increase in the number of people setting up online businesses has meant that there's greater competition. But with clarity of focus and better systems you can set yourself apart from the many me-too-kind of businesses on the net.

> "The new information technology, Internet and e-mail, have practically eliminated the physical costs of communications."
>
> **Peter Drucker**

Apply the same process of preparation that is needed to go into any kind of business when you start your online business. Know your target market, know your differentiating factors and clarify your processes. Then start looking at the technical aspects like hosting, domain names, website design and payment processors. It is now possible to get very affordable hosting that will come with a domain name, website development tools and even a payment processor. Look for quality at a low price; trust me it does exist in the online market. You also need to spend time, energy and money on marketing; just building a fancy website won't get you customers. You can read up on online marketing that works and apply some of the principles that are out there.

8. What If I Can't Manage Finances?

Financial management is key to business success, so what if you don't know anything about finances. You can institute a few measures to make sure you are not setting yourself up for failure.

Firstly appoint a financial officer or an accountant to help you with your financial management. Some business structures such as corporation and company have this as a requirement. You can have an accountant on a needs-based arrangement where you only pay them for what they do. Secondly, get yourself an accounting software program that will help you invoice your customers and track your finances on a day-to-day basis. Accounting software has made financial management simpler for the rest of us. If you get the more expensive packages you can create elaborate reports with a touch of a button and look like a pro even if you're a rookie.

9. What If I Can't Price Right?

The prices you charge for what you sell have an enormous ability to affect your company's growth. You need to charge enough to cover costs, but keep prices low enough to attract customers. How do you balance that equation from get-go? Pricing too low can attract some customers but can also drive others away. So you've got to decide which customers are you going for as this will affect your pricing strategy. Your competition will also affect your pricing. Your customers have an option to shop around and they surely use it like you do.

Try to keep your costs down so that your mark up can always be comfortable for your profitability. Finding the right spot between your cost and the highest price customers will tolerate, given existing competition will take time to perfect. Do not let your competition define you but rather find a way to become a standard that others in your field follow.

10.   What If I Need To Hire Help?

Your business has grown; you can't be the receptionist, sales person and company president all at once anymore. How do you go about hiring help that you need to run your business successfully? Before you hire see if you can outsource. Outsourcing means you get another company to handle certain elements of your business on a needs basis. You can get a great phone answering service for a lot less than a salary for a receptionist. This will work up to a certain point then you'll need to start hiring.

Here is what to do when you do hire employees. Have clear roles and job descriptions and proper contracts drawn up. Start with short-term contracts 3-6 months with an option to renew, this will safe guard you if you make a mistake in hiring. Don't hire the first person that comes your way. Ask for recommendations from people you trust and know. Study your candidates' backgrounds and history carefully so that you're not caught unaware when you've already hired. Decide to pay fairly and you'll get the right candidates too.

11.   What If My Idea Doesn't Work?

The hardest thing for any entrepreneur to deal with is a failed business idea. You put your sweat into it; you sacrifice for it and after a while in some cases you have to admit that your idea is not working. What must you do in such cases?

> "Failure is the opportunity to begin again, more intelligently."
>
> Henry Ford

As hard as it may be do not hold on to an idea that is not working, sure evaluate it, change the strategy and try again. But when you realise that it is really not working, count your losses early and hang it up. The sooner you give up on a bad idea the better, as this will stop you from wrecking your future business successes. Do not let a failed business idea get you off the track of entrepreneurship.

The successful young entrepreneur is a serial entrepreneur. He/she understands like Richard Branson that one failed idea is the training ground for the one that will make you rich beyond your dreams.

So there you are! Hopefully now you will feel equipped to make your mark in the entrepreneur world. I took the step into entrepreneurship and it changed my life. I had some good ideas and some really bad ones. The good ones made me money and the bad ones took some of that money away but I had a good sense to give up on the bad before they wrecked my chances with the good.

You have what it takes to be a successful entrepreneur. Please do not waste too much of your time with some of the get rich quick schemes disguised as online businesses, they will eat up your money and leave you despondent. Rather work on your own ideas, or improve on someone else's idea that works for your own market.

Go and be successful! You can do it!

RESOURCES:

Where To Find More Information And Guidance

*H*ere are a few pointers to resources and places to go for support and guidance:

YoungEntrepreneur.co.za –
www.youngentrepreneur.co.za
This is a great blog by Buhle Dlamini for you entrepreneurs with information and links to various resources and websites.

Business Owner's Toolkit
http://www.toolkit.cch.com/
CCH Incorporated provides a brief overview of financing basics: Debts vs. Equity. The basic types of financing assist users with understanding, which

options might be most attractive and realistically available to their particular business.

The Business Start Page
http://www.bspage.com/

The Business Start Page is suggested by its author as a page from which the business owner can launch his work on the Internet, rather than "surfing" around trying to find useful business information. The page has little original content but is regularly updated and contains links useful to business people. A section called The Virtual Desk links to phone and business directories and general reference tools. The Reference Library has links to business reference sources and other sections are featured with subjects deemed by the author to be of interest to small business owners.

CCH Business Owner's Toolkit
http://www.toolkit.com/

A resource for small business owners that covers topics like starting your business and managing finances. Provides access to a wide variety of business tools, including forms and model business plans. The section of the site that offers business reports and trademark/patent searches requires registration and fees.

Center for Business Planning
http://www.businessplans.org/

"The Center for Business Planning provides any business manager or entrepreneur with a set of resources to help in creating a business or managing a business. Information is provided on every area of planning a business including: acquire venture capital, define new products, market analysis, competitive analysis, production management, tax problems, legal issues, prepare financial statements, write a business plan and much more."

BizJam for SA's Young Entrepreneurs
http://www.bizjam.co.za

Provides a great platform for connecting young entrepreneurs to each other. It is absolutely awesome for networking, finding business partners and marketing too. It has blogs and other social networking capabilities.

ENTERWeb: The Enterprise Development
http://www.enterweb.org/

ENTERWeb: The Enterprise Development Website is a portal for information on enterprise development, international trade, finance, and economics.

Entrepreneur's Library
http://www.caycon.com/resources.php

This is a directory of resources including articles and websites developed specifically to assist entrepreneurs get their businesses off the ground.

Entrepreneurs' Help Page
http://www.tannedfeet.com/

"This site is designed, created, and published by a group of young professionals. We put together our skills and knowledge to publish this site to help out other young people or inexperienced business people with good ideas and the desire to start their own business. This web site distributes basic information on legal, financial, and management issues that commonly affect (or afflict!) people who are just starting up their businesses." Extensive articles on opening and financing a business. Legal resources on incorporation, intellectual property, taxation, contracts, and links to legal forms. New content added often.

FindLaw for Small Business
http://smallbusiness.findlaw.com/

General and legal information relevant to small businesses. Its "Self Help Legal Guides" on topics such as "Business Formation", "Business Planning", "Finance", and "Human Resources" include articles, web links, FAQs and forms.

Free Management Library
http://www.managementhelp.org/
The Free Management Library provides extensive how-to management information to managers -- particularly those with very limited resources. Items in the library are relevant to both for-profit and nonprofit organizations unless otherwise marked at the top of the page containing the item. Organized into 675 different management related categories, the library provides resources from topics ranging from organizational communitation to e-commerce to risk management.

How To Guides for Starting and Running a Business
http://www.entrepreneur.com/howto/ Resources on starting a business, money, management, marketing, sales, advertising, human resources, and technology from Entrepreneur.com.

Inc.com
http://www.inc.com/home/index.html
Inc.com contains resources, handpicked by Inc.com editors, on specific business-management issues. Use them to discover strategies for starting, growing, and running your business more effectively and successfully.

Kauffman eVenturing: The Entrepreneur's Trusted Guide to High Growth
http://eventuring.kauffman.org

"Provides original articles, written by entrepreneurs for entrepreneurs, and aggregates "the best of the best" content on the Web related to starting and running high-impact companies."

Managing a Small Business
http://www.liraz.com/

This site, from a commercial publisher of business books and CD-ROMs, has useful articles and tips for small business owners, many of which are excerpts from the company's products, but are meaty enough to be useful online. Tips on goal setting, managing people, managing yourself, being an entrepreneur, planning, markcting, cutting expenses, and more.

Online Women's Business Center
http://www.onlinewbc.gov/

"This interactive business skills training web site is dedicated to helping entrepreneurial women to realize their goals and aspirations for their personal and professional development. Our goal is to provide them with the information and expertise necessary for planning their economic independence through owning their own business." The information includes online forums, message boards, as well as resource databases and informative articles. The site is searchable and is available in English, Spanish, and Russian.

Restaurant Report
http://www.restaurantreport.com/
Catering to the independent restaurant owner, this site provides information on restaurant management as well as tips on how to deliver "outstanding local dining experiences!" Restaurant Report is a sister site to RunningRestaurants.com and is the publisher of a major industry e-newsletter. Offers a wealth of information, including: 25 top ranked industry websites, a buyer's guide, links to products and services, an events calendar, an online store, and articles on restaurant ownership and management.

Startup Company Valuation Calculator
http://www.caycon.com/valuation.php
This is an educational and humorous multiple-choice quiz for estimating the value of an early-stage company.

Strategis
http://strategis.ic.gc.ca/engdoc/main.html
A website about Canadian business put out by the Minister of Industry. The site has sections on company information, international business,

consumer information, technology, business support, human resources, small businesses, and more. Versions of the site are available in English or French.

U. S. Small Business Administration
http://www.sba.gov/

Get information here on the U.S. Small Business Administration programs and publications about starting, financing, and expanding a small business. The SBA, established in 1953, provides financial, technical and management assistance to help Americans start, run, and grow their businesses. With a portfolio of business loans, loan guarantees and disaster loans worth more than $45 billion, in addition to a venture capital portfolio of $13 billion, SBA is the nation's largest single financial backer of small businesses. Last year, the SBA offered management and technical assistance to more than one million small business owners. The SBA also plays a major role in the government's disaster relief efforts by making low-interest recovery loans to both homeowners and businesses.

EnterpriseSA – Business Support
http://www.enterprisesa.com/za

One of South Africa's leading business support websites. Users can register and have access to the amazing business tools. Users can make a business plan, view sample plans, calculate starting costs, and more.

Buhle Dlamini is an entrepreneur, a sought-after professional speaker, author and managing director of Young and Able cc, a personal and business development consultancy. He is the publisher of *Motivated.co.za* and *YoungEntrepreneur.co.za* that both have thousands of members from around the globe. He helps organisations and individuals to activate their potential and in so doing, contributes to the development of the next generation of leaders. Apart from running his own business, he is also a strategic partner to *Heartlines*, a mass-media initiative promoting sound values, which aired on SABC, South African National TV. With Heartlines they recently launched the *Heartlines Youth Mentors Initiative* encouraging South Africans to mentor young people for good.

Buhle's strategic input on business and leading the next generation of employees and talent has been employed by some of the top blue chip companies nationally and internationally. His business website is at **www.youngable.com**

www.ingramcontent.com/pod-product-compliance
Lightning Source LLC
Chambersburg PA
CBHW071226170526
45165CB00003B/1011